Around the World with KoKo

Dana Copeland

Front Cover Illustrated by:
Ana K. Quintero V.

Published By:
Alabaster Box, LLC

Dedicated to:

My nieces Kymari and Kailaya,
Always follow your dreams,
wherever they may take you.

Egypt and the people
I know and cherish.
You will **always** have my heart.
Please accept this as
my timeless love letter to you.
I'll see you again, **أن شاء الله**.

Love you most,
KoKo

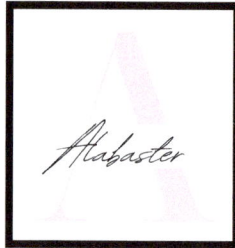

Alabaster

First Edition, 2022
ISBN 979-8-9859157-3-0

Published by: Alabaster Box, LLC
www.danacopeland.com

Table of Contents

Introduction

Dear Kymari and Kailaya,

Wow! That was a LONG plane ride! Florida is so far away from Egypt! Egypt is a country on the **continent** of Africa.

I can't wait until you're old enough to travel with me! I can teach you some **Arabic** words to use by then. **Arabic** is the official language in Egypt, although many people speak French and English.

Did you know there's a **time difference** here? We'll have to schedule our calls around it; when you get out of school, it'll almost be time for me to go to bed! I wish you were here.

Love you most,
KoKo

Did You Know?

Egypt is the 12th largest country in Africa and about twice the size of France. It's HUGE!

France

Egypt

The view on my first flight to Egypt

Fun Facts

- Florida is about 6,468 mi (10,409 km) from Egypt!
- There are almost five times as many people living in Egypt compared to Florida.
- There are no direct flights from Florida to Egypt. I want that to change. ⌣

Welcome to Maadi

Ky and Kai,
   Guess what? I found an apartment! I live in **Cairo**. My place is in a small district of Cairo called **Maadi**.
   When I told people I was moving to Egypt, they assumed I would live somewhere in the middle of the desert LOL, but the streets of **Maadi** have tall trees and beautiful flowers.

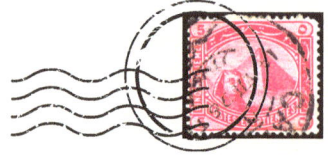

Love you most,
KoKo

Kymari and Kailaya
231 Bears Street
Auburndale, FL 33823

Cairo is the capital of Egypt.

There are many **expats** or people who live in a different country than where they were born, in Maadi.

Sunset in **Maadi**

My neighborhood

Fun Fact

They gave us some **Egyptian Pounds** today. That is the official currency in Egypt, but the U.S. Dollar is worth more. I'm not used to hearing that something costs 250 **Egyptian Pounds,** which is only about $15!

My apartment in **Maadi**

Egyptian Pounds

Beautiful **Maadi**

7

Pyramids of Giza

Dear Kymari and Kailaya,

   As soon as I walked outside, it felt like I was in an oven. The hot and dry **climate** of the **Sahara Desert** is too much for me! As we drove past the longest river in the world, The **Nile River**, I wished I could jump in and take a swim.

   Seeing **The Pyramids of Giza**, one of the Seven Wonders of the Ancient World was one of the best days of my life! Did you know you can go inside some of the pyramids? Ancient Egyptians built them as **tombs** for

Physical Map of Egypt

pharaohs. They believed that if you preserved a dead person's body through **mummification**, their soul would live on forever.

   Although not all pyramids are in Giza, the third-largest city in Egypt, it houses the largest pyramid in Egypt, **The Great Pyramid of Khufu.** I promise to bring you here one day! You'll love it so much!

Love you most,
   KoKo

Answer: C

Dinner with a view

Tourist poses with
The **Sphinx**

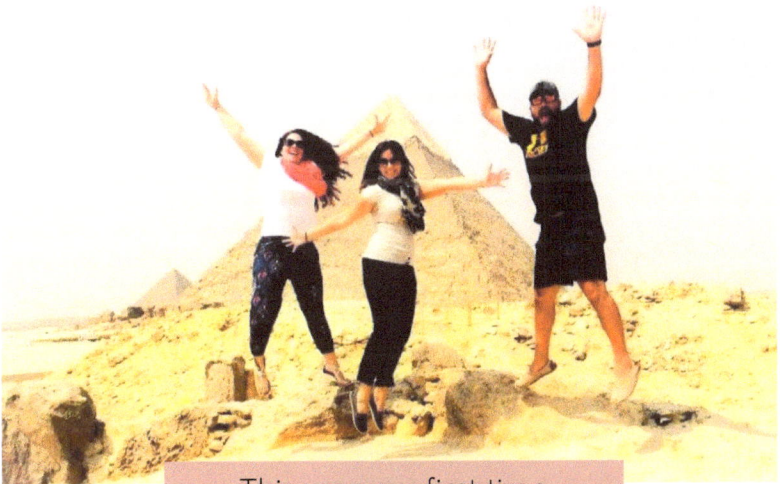

This was my first time
at the pyramids.

Pyramids and Sphinx

The Great Pyramid of Giza

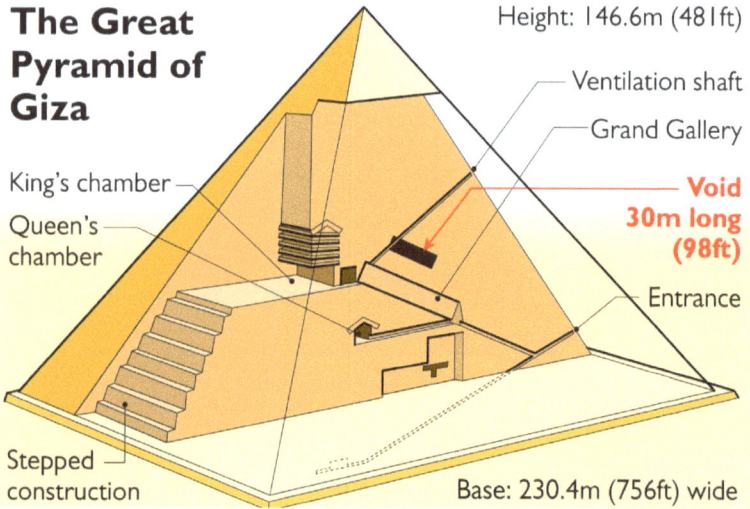

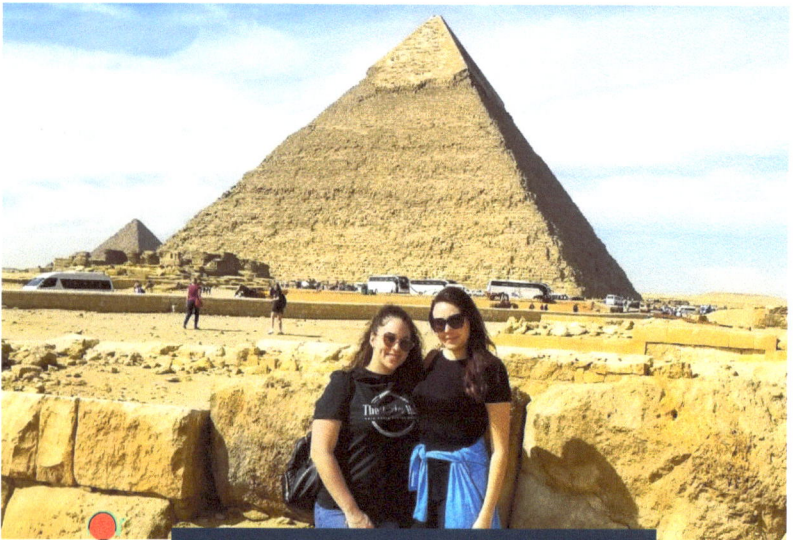

Height: 146.6m (481ft)

Ventilation shaft

Grand Gallery

Void 30m long (98ft)

King's chamber

Queen's chamber

Entrance

Stepped construction

Base: 230.4m (756ft) wide

The Great Pyramid of Khafre or "The Great Pyramid of Giza"

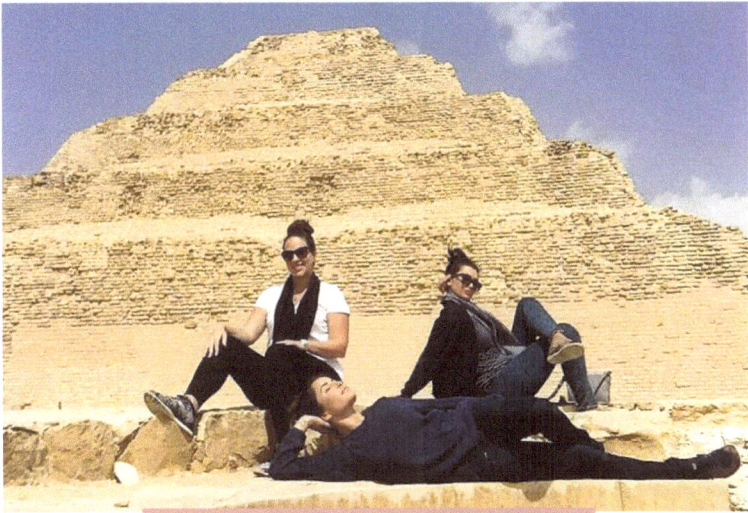

The **Step Pyramid of Djoser** is located in Saqqara, Egypt.

Dear Kymari and Kailaya,

When I finally crawled my way inside the pyramid, I thought I'd see some extraordinary treasures, but most of the items were stolen long ago. I wonder what it looked like when they first built these ancient structures.

With a length of 240 feet (73 m) and a height of 66 feet (20 m), The **Sphinx** is one of the largest sculptures in the world. It has a lion's body and the head of a human decorated with a royal headdress. It took many years to uncover and restore most of the Sphinx. Its missing nose is still a mystery. What do you think happened to it?

Love you most,
KoKo

Camels

Dear Kymari and Kailaya,
    You already know what my favorite animal is, but did you know…

- Many people think camels store water in their humps, but they store fat.
- They can store up to 80 pounds of fat and go weeks or even months without eating.
- When a camel finally finds water, it can drink up to 40 gallons at a time!

Camel kisses are the best kisses!

Fun Fact

Camels have three sets of eyelids and two rows of eyelashes to keep all the sand out of their eyes!

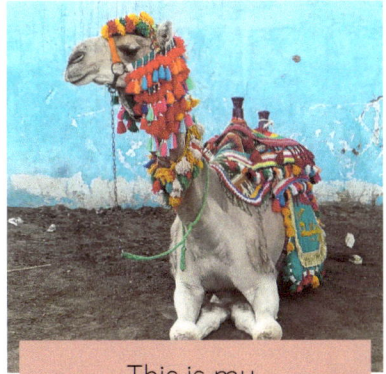

This is my **FAVORITE** animal!

Their average total height is 7 ft. (2.13 m) and they live for approximately 40-50 years.

Tombs and Temples

Abydos **Temples**

Medinet Habu **Temple**

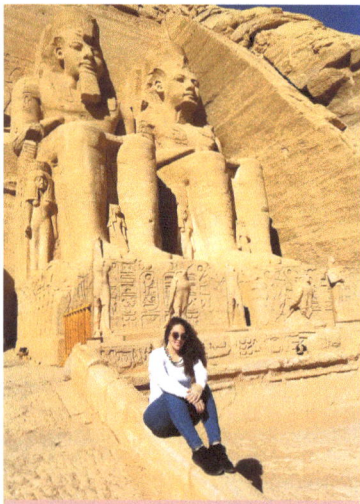

Abu Simbel Temples

Dear Kymari and Kailaya,

I can't believe the things I saw in the cities of Luxor and Aswan. Look at how the pharaohs are cut into the rocks at **Abu Simbel**. How did they make these masterpieces? The statues are 69 feet (21 m) tall, about the same height as the columns in the **Karnak Temple**.

The **temples** were so detailed! Can you believe that you can still see some of the colors they used on the **hieroglyphics** inside the **temples** thousands of years ago?

These are just a few of my favorite **temples,** but there are many more I'll take you to.

Love you most,
KoKo

Karnak Temple

The Nile River

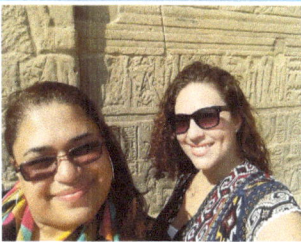

My Travel Partner

According to the Ancient Egyptians, every **temple** was dedicated to specific gods or goddesses, and they were worshiped there.

The **temples** are on the East Bank of the **Nile River**, and the **tombs** are on the West Bank. They did this because the Sun rises in the East, representing life, and it sets in the West, representing death.

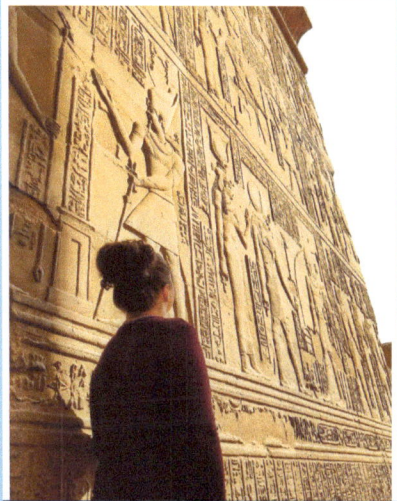

The **Temple** of Edfu, also known as The **Temple** of Horus

The Black and White Deserts

Sunset in the **White Desert**

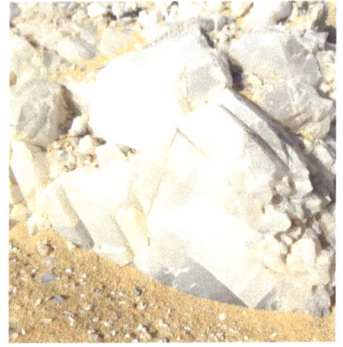

Colorless crystals
in the **White Desert**

We went sand
surfing in the desert.

The Black Desert

Camping under
the stars. Have you ever
seen so many in the sky?

The **White Desert** is known for its white, chalk formations.

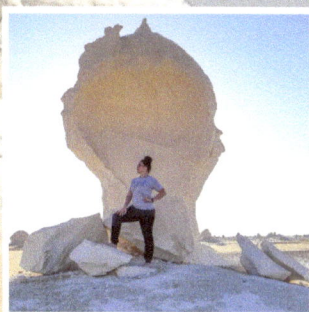

We were about to race through the desert.

Dear Kymari and Kailaya,

There are parts of Egypt that are not visited as much by tourists. They are called the **Black and White Deserts**. They make you feel like you are on another planet! The **Black Desert** has volcano-shaped mounds covered by a fine, dark-colored rock. You also have to see Crystal Mountain! It's about 18 mi (30 km) outside the Black Desert and covered with colorless crystals. The **White Desert** is one of the most incredible places I've ever explored. Which one do you want to visit first?

Love you most,
KoKo

17

Landforms and Bodies of Water

Dear Kymari and Kailaya,

  I love that Egypt has so many different landforms and bodies of water! I just returned from a beach trip to Dahab and Sharm El Sheikh. We got to see the most beautiful fish and coral in the crystal clear water. You could even see Saudi Arabia across the Gulf of Aqaba. Egypt has so much to offer. People come from all around the world to visit their incredible beaches and scuba dive in Egypt.
  I went snorkeling, rode an ATV by the mountains, and then had dinner by camels in the desert! What more could I ask for in a country? I LOVE it here!
  We just booked a trip to hike **Mount Sinai** with my friends. Wish me luck! I can't wait to explore more of this beautiful country.

Love you most,
KoKo

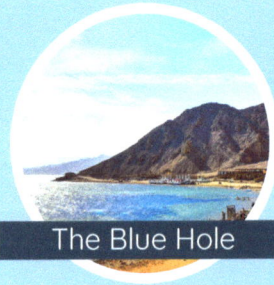

The Blue Hole

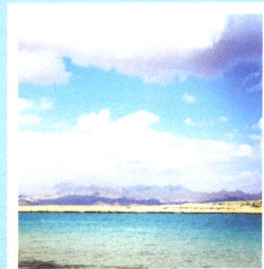

Ras Mohammad

Fun Facts

The Blue Hole is located in the Red Sea, which is home to around 1,200 fish species and 250 coral species.

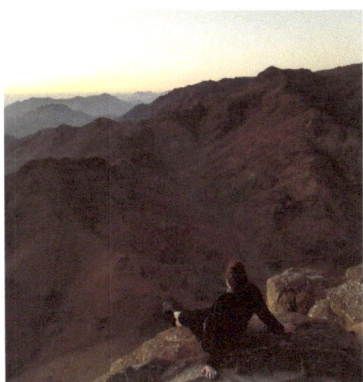

Dear Kymari and Kailaya,
   I didn't think I was going to make it to the top of **Mount Sinai** because at 7,497 feet (2,285 m) above sea level, it became harder to breathe, but I would gladly go again if I could do it with the two of you!
                    Love you most,
                    KoKo

The best adventures are with friends.

We hiked **Mount Sinai** to watch the sunrise.

Khan El Khalili

A papyrus painting

Dear Kymari and Kailaya,

The **Khan el Khalili** is an outdoor market known as a bazaar or souk. It reminds me of one of our favorite movies. I'll give you a hint. We saw the remake together, and there's a monkey in it. Can you guess the movie? I bought you a lamp as a souvenir to remind you of it.

There were SO many people there, and it was extremely crowded. They sell art, food, jewelry, souvenirs, spices, perfume, and more! I was even able to see how they made **papyrus** paper from the reeds of the **papyrus** plant. I felt overwhelmed by the people, different noises, and smells, but you can't visit Egypt without going there.

Love you most,
KoKo

Papyrus paper

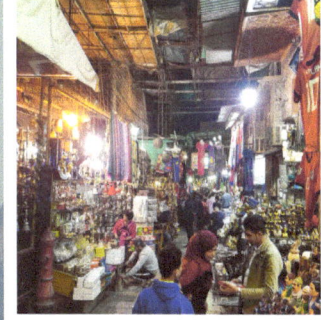

Facts about the Khan

- You can bargain because most shops do not have set prices.
- It was built over 600 years ago!
- It's located in the heart of Islamic **Cairo** near several **mosques**.

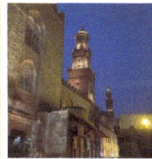

Mosques and Churches

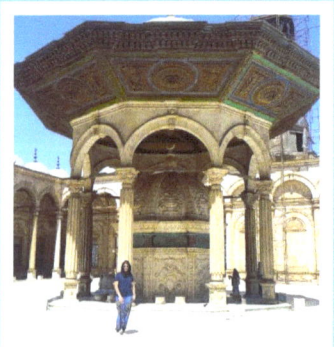

Dear Kymari and Kailaya,

I've visited some beautiful mosques in Egypt. **Mosques** are the places of worship for **Muslims**, like the church is for Christians. Some of the prettiest and most elaborately designed places I've seen in the world are **mosques**. They are so peaceful and beautiful. It's a fantastic place to visit and pray. These are some of my favorites in Egypt.

Love you most,
KoKo

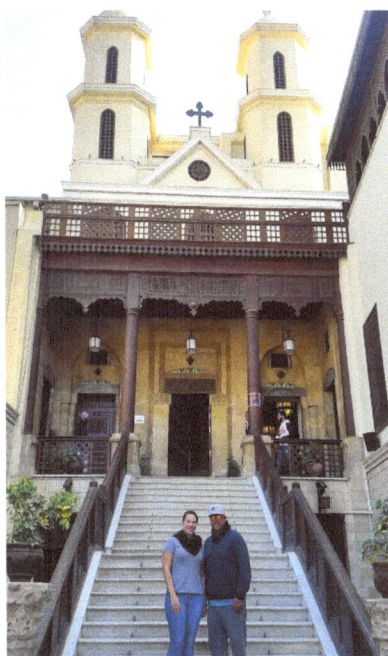

Saint Simon Church, or "The Cave Church," is named after St. Simon, who was able to move the mountain because of his strong faith. It sits over 20,000 people and is located in an area called "Garbage City."

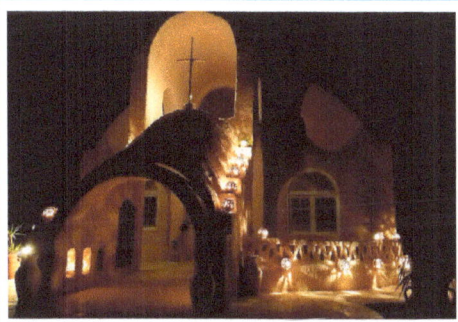

One of my favorite churches in Egypt.

Food and Holidays

Dear Kymari and Kailaya,

Egypt has some of the BEST food I've ever tasted!
I have to be careful because many of their meals include rice and bread, and I can quickly overeat. I don't know what it is about their rice, but it's the best I've ever tasted! I can't wait to make some of my favorite dishes for you.

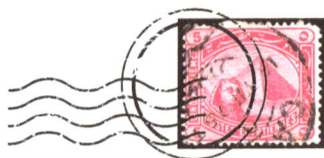

Love you most,
KoKo

Kymari and Kailaya
231 Bears Street
Auburndale, FL 33823

Mixed Grill

Basbousa

Molokhia

Lemon-Mint drink

Koshary

Ta'ameya (or Falafel)

There are many celebrations and holidays in Egypt, like **Eid El Fitr**, Revolution Day, Coptic Christmas, and many others, but my favorite is **Ramadan**.

The streets and cities are covered with bright and colorful decorations. I like to hang a **fanoos**, or colorful lantern, in my apartment. **Ramadan** is a month of fasting, prayer, reflection, and community. I love to participate in it with my students and neighbors. It's fun to learn more about other people's cultures!

Dates are eaten to break daily **Ramadan** fasts.

Fanoos sale

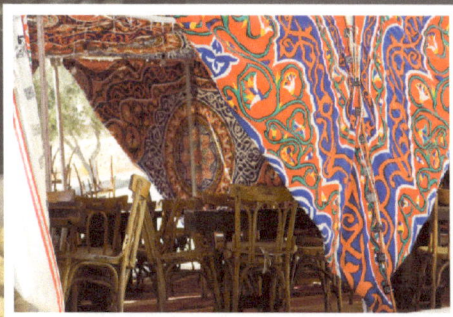

This is a **Ramadan** tent where people go to eat Iftar, the meal they eat after sunset, together.

All About Egypt

The Egyptian flag

It has the Mediterranean Sea to the north and the Red Sea to the east.

This is a **political map** of Africa. It shows the borders of all its countries and major cities.

Can you use the compass rose to find the countries to the west and south of Egypt?

Fun Facts

← This is my **Arabic** workbook.

- **Arabic** is the official language in 25 countries.
- **Arabic** is read from right to left, except numbers.
- **Arabic** has sounds that don't exist in other languages.

Galabeya

Abaya

Hijab

Dear Kymari and Kailaya,

Many people think all women wear a hijab or abaya in Egypt and men or women wear galabeyas, but that's not true; some wear similar clothes to you and me.

Arabic has been a difficult language for me to learn, but I love talking to my friends and locals in their native language. I enjoy taking Arabic classes, and I'll teach you all of the Arabic I know one day, أن شاء الله. (Insha'Allah, if it's God's will).

♡ Love you most,
KoKo

27

Fun Facts

1

Ancient Egyptians used **hieroglyphics** as their alphabet. There are over 700 hieroglyphs! Can you spot some of them in the book?

Pg. 15, 28, 35

2

About 90% of Egyptians are **Muslims**, which means they are followers of **Islam**. About 10% of Egyptians are **Coptic Christians**.

3

Egypt is divided into 2 sections: Upper Egypt (Southern Egypt) and Lower Egypt (Northern Egypt). They're named that because the Nile River flows from South to North.

4

Each stone block of the pyramid weighs about 5,000 pounds (2,267 kg)!

5

About 104 million people live in Egypt! It is the third most populated country in Africa after Nigeria and Ethiopia.

6

The Great Pyramid of **Khufu** is the largest Egyptian pyramid. It weighs as much as 16 Empire State Buildings!

7

Ancient Egyptians invented the door lock, toothpaste, breath mints, the plow, the calendar, paper, the written language, and eye makeup, to name a few things.

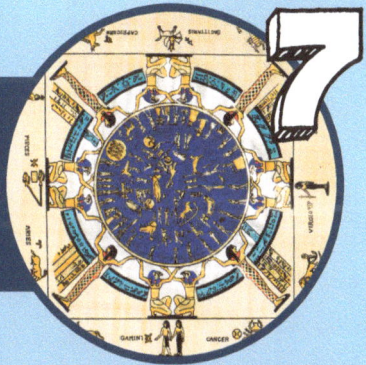

8

The most popular sport in Egypt is football. We call it soccer in the United States. Do you know who the most famous football player from Egypt is?

Answer: Mohamed Salah

Show What You Know

1

What is the name of the largest pyramid in Egypt?

A. The Step Pyramid of Djoser
B. The Great Pyramid of Khufu
C. The Pyramid of Teti
D. The Bent Pyramid

2

How many people live in Egypt?

A. 23 million
B. 57 million
C. 104 million
D. 86 million

3

What is the official currency in Egypt?

A. Dollar
B. Pounds
C. Dinar
D. Euro

What is the official language in Egypt?

A. Arabic
B. English
C. Zulu
D. Thai

What is the average overall height of a camel?

A. 9 feet
B. 5 feet
C. 4 feet
D. 7 feet

What is the name of the place where Muslims worship?

A. Mosque
B. Temple
C. Church
D. Synagogue

Answers 1.B, 2.C, 3.B, 4.A, 5.D, 6.A

31

Glossary

Abaya
a loose garment worn
by some Muslim women

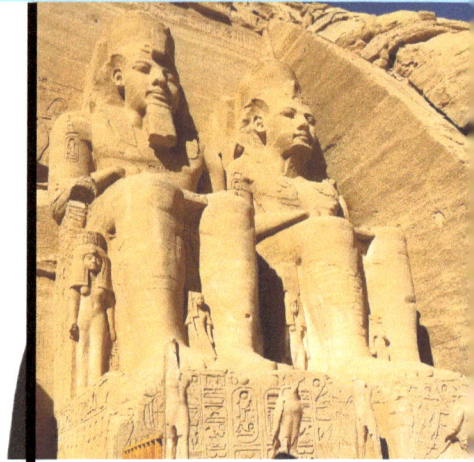

Abu Simbel
the site of two temples
built into the rocks

Black Desert
a region in Egypt with volcano-
shaped mounds that are topped
with fine, dark-colored rocks

Blue Hole
a famous diving location
in the Sinai Peninsula

Arabic
the official language of Egypt

Basbousa
A sweet, semolina cake soaked in a flavored syrup

Cairo
the capital city of Egypt

Climate
the average weather conditions in a place over many years

Glossary

Continent
one of the seven major
landmasses in the world

Coptic Christian
a person that lives in
Egypt and follows Christianity

Expat
or an expatriate, is a person
who lives in a different country
than where they were born

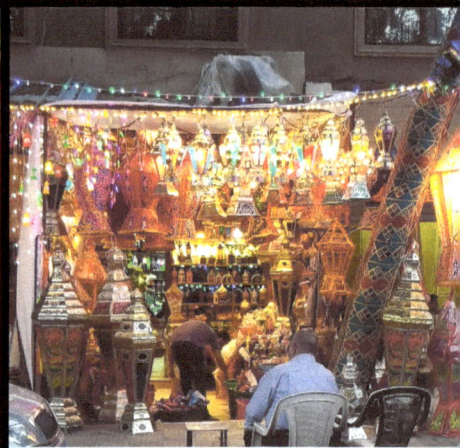

Fanoos
a type of lantern used for
Ramadan decorations

Egyptian Pound
the official currency of Egypt

Eid El Fitr
a holiday that celebrates the end of Ramadan

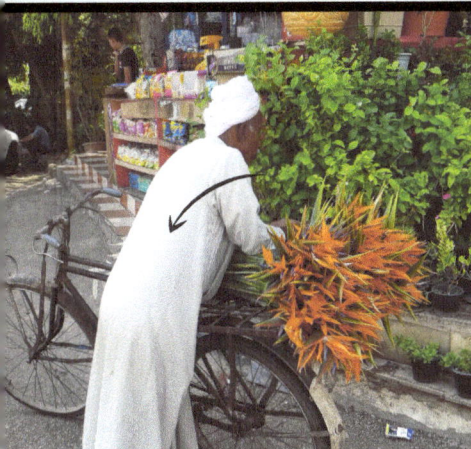

Galabeya
a loose fitting garment worn by men and women in Egypt

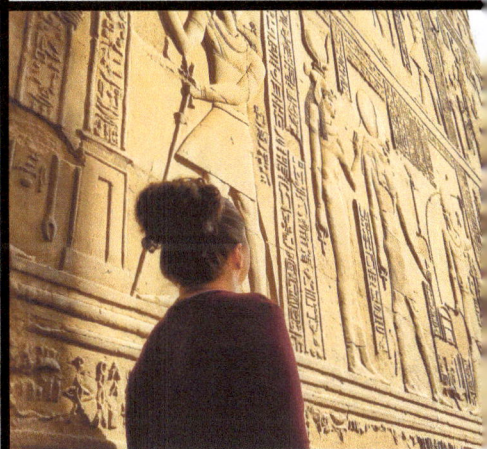

Hieroglyphics
a form or writing that uses pictures and is found on walls of temples, tombs, and papyrus

Glossary

Hijab
a head scarf worn by some Muslim women

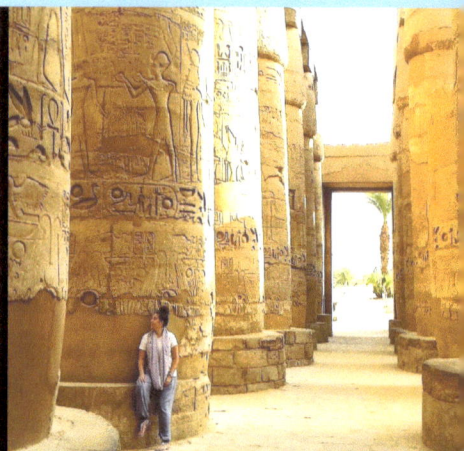

Karnak Temple
a large temple located on the banks of the Nile River

Maadi
a small district of Cairo

Mixed Grill
a meal consisting of grilled meats and vegetables

Khan el Khalili
a famous market in Cairo, known as a souk or bazaar

Koshary
a popular dish with pasta, lentils, and rice, topped with a tomato sauce and fried onions

Molokhia
made using the minced leaves of a Molokhia plant and is cooked with spices in broth

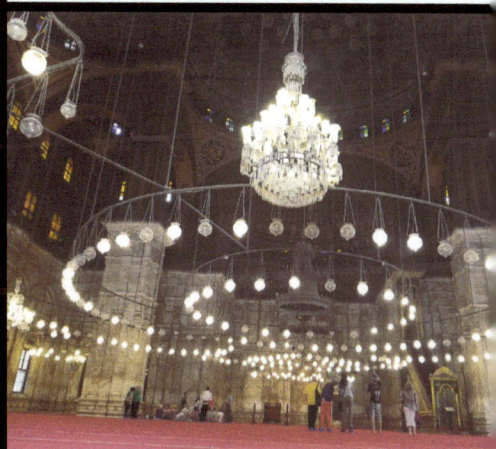

Mosque
the place of worship for people that follow Islam (Muslims)

Glossary

Mount Sinai
a mountain in the Sinai Peninsula, known as the place where Moses received the Ten Commandments

Mummification
a way to prepare a body after death so it does not decay

Pharaohs
the queens and kings of Ancient Egypt

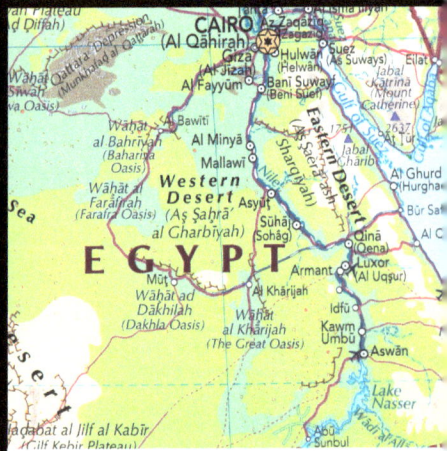

Physical Map
a map that shows the features of an area such as landforms or bodies of water

Nile River
the longest river in the world

Papyrus
the original form of paper invented by Ancient Egyptians from the papyrus plant

Political Map
shows the boundaries of states and countries, as well as cities and capitals

Ramadan
a month of fasting, prayer, reflection, and community for Muslims

Glossary

Sahara Desert
the largest hot desert in the world and it covers most of Egypt

Sphinx
a limestone structure that has a lion's body and a human head decorated with a royal headdress

The Pyramids of Giza
the 3 main pyramids of the Pharaohs Khufu, Khafre, and Menkaure

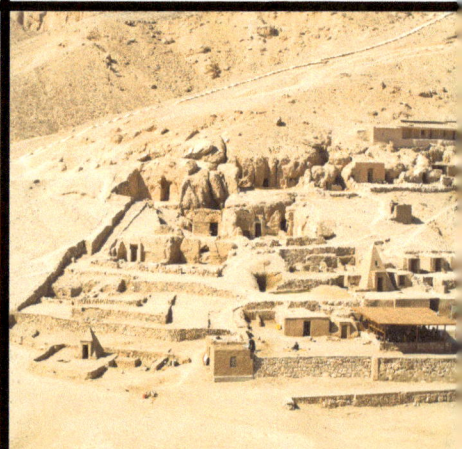

Tombs
a place where people were buried in Ancient Egypt

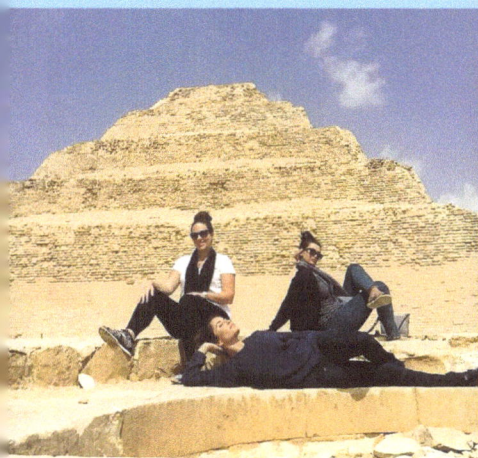

Step Pyramid of Djoser
the oldest pyramid in Egypt,
located in Saqqara, Egypt

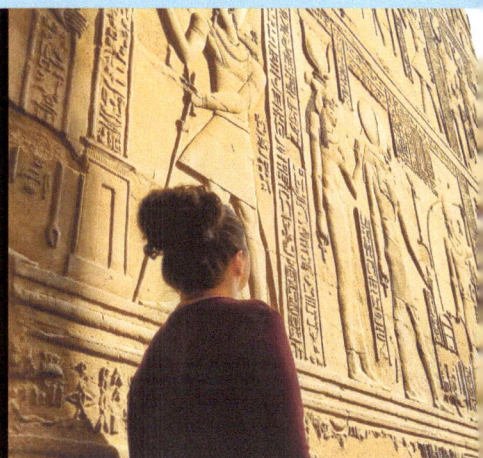

Temple
the place to worship
gods and goddesses

Time difference
the difference in time in various
time zones around the world

White Desert
a desert that is made of
white chalk-like formations

Koshary Recipe

Ingredients

Koshary
- 1 cup of rice, rinsed and drained
- 1 cup of brown lentils rinsed and drained
- 1/2 cup of vermicelli pasta
- 1/2 cup of circle or elbow noodles
- 1 15-oz can of chickpeas, drained

Tomato Sauce
- 1 28-oz can of tomato sauce
- 1 tsp onion powder (or to taste)
- 3 minced garlic cloves
- 1 Tbsp vegetable oil
- 2 Tbsp of ground coriander (or to taste)
- 2 tbsp ground cumin (or to taste)
- 1/2-1 tsp red pepper flakes
- 1 Tbsp distilled white vinegar
- Salt and pepper

Crispy Onion Toppings
- 1 large onion cut into thin slices
- 1/2 cup all-purpose flour
- 1/2 vegetable oil
- Salt to taste

Directions

Koshary

1. Boil the rice, lentils, noodles, and vermicelli pasta separately according to the directions on the package and flavor with salt. Set aside.
2. Cook the chickpeas until they are warm (with a little bit of water, so they don't saute), and then season with salt and pepper.

Tomato Sauce

1. Saute the garlic in oil until it becomes fragrant.
2. Add the tomato sauce and the rest of the ingredients. Bring to a simmer and remove from the heat.

Crispy Onion Toppings

1. After slicing the onions, cut them in flour and salt. Shake off the excess flour.
2. Cook them until brown and crispy on both sides.

Time for the Magic

1. Layer all of the Koshary ingredients or combine them.
2. Add tomato sauce and top with crispy onions.
3. Enjoy.

Arabic Lesson

Numbers

٠	١	٢	٣	٤
zero	one	two	three	four

٥	٦	٧	٨	٩
five	six	seven	eight	nine

example: 231, ٢٣١ ⟵   I used to live on Street ٢٣١ in Maadi.

Fun Fact

I teach my students how to say common phrases and write numbers in Arabic now that I'm teaching in the United States. They love it!

44

Vocabulary Words

If God wills or God willing	*In-sha-Allah* **Insha'Allah**	أن شاء الله
"How are you?" (to a female)	*iz-zI-Eek?* **Ezzayek**	ازيك
"How are you?" (to a male)	iz-zI-ak **Ezzayak?**	ازيك
"Goodbye."	Ma-el-Sala-ma **MaAa el Salama**	مع السلامة
"Thank you"	Show-kron **Shokran**	شكراً
"No thank you."	Lah show-kron **La, Shokran**	لا ، شكرا
"You're welcome"	Af-won **Afwan**	عفواً
"Let's go." or "Come on."	Yal-lah **Yalla**	يلا

45

Index

Nonfiction Scavenger Hunt

Fact or Opinion?

Find 3 facts and 3 opinions from the text.

Write 3 opinions of your own based on our trip to Egypt.

Text Features

Use the text to find an example of:

- a heading
- a label
- a caption
- bold print
- a photograph
- a diagram
- a map
- the glossary

Captions

Choose two photographs from the book and create your own captions.

46

Flight Details

What country should we explore next?

Submit your answer to aroundtheworldwithkoko@gmail.com

Websites

The following websites were used for the facts presented on page(s):

4- https://www.mylifeelsewhere.com/country-size-comparison/egypt/france
https://en.wikipedia.org/wiki/List_of_African_countries_by_area
5- https://www.freemaptools.com/how-far-is-it-between.htm
https://www.populationu.com/us/florida-population
5, 29, and 30- https://www.macrotrends.net/countries/EGY/egypt/population
8- https://en.wikipedia.org/wiki/Egyptian_pyramids
https://worldpopulationreview.com/countries/cities/egypt
10- https://www.thetimes.co.uk/article/mystery-void-found-in-great-pyramid-of-giza-d002hr6kf, **Image Credit:** https://www.thetimes.co.uk/article/mystery-void-found-in-great-pyramid-of-giza-d002hr6kf
11 and 41-https://www.britannica.com/topic/Great-Sphinx,
https://easyscienceforkids.com/the-great-sphinx-of-giza-fun-facts/
12- https://spana.org/blog/13-fun-facts-about-camels/
13 and 31- https://www.mvorganizing.org/how-wide-are-camels/
14- https://flyandsea.com/10-interesting-facts-about-egypt-the-red-sea/
15- https://www.britannica.com/place/Mount-Sinai-mountain-Egypt
16- **Image Credit:** Christian Reynolds Photography
17- https://www.thetravelersbuddy.com/2020/07/14/black-white-desert-egypt/
19- https://www.traveltoegypt.net/discover-egypt/cairo-attractions/khan-el-khalili
20- https://www.livescience.com/37360-abu-simbel.html,
https://www.memphis.edu/hypostyle/tour_hall/great_columns.php
21- http://www.ancientegypt.co.uk/temples/home.html
23- https://www.gospelherald.com/articles/64933/20160627/cave-church-in-egypt
27- https://worldpopulationreview.com/country-rankings/arabic-speaking-countries
28- https://www.yac-uk.org/news/fun-facts-hierolglyphs
https://culturalatlas.sbs.com.au/egyptian-culture/egyptian-culture-religion
29- https://www.worldometers.info/population/countries-in-africa-by-population/
https://www.dkfindout.com/us/history/ancient-egypt/inside-great-pyramid/
https://science.howstuffworks.com/innovation/inventions/5-amazing-ancient-egyptian-inventions
30 and 40- https://www.britannica.com/topic/Pyramids-of-Giza

About the Author

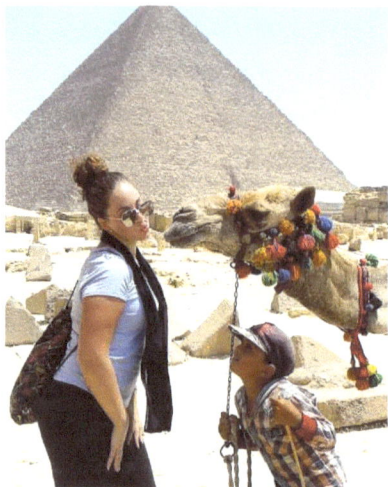

Dana Copeland was born and raised in Florida. She has been a teacher for 13 years. She first fell in love with Egypt in the 3rd grade after completing a class project on Africa. She dreamed of one day visiting the country full of ancient wonders and so much history.

In 2015, her dream came true. Although many questioned her timing because her sister had just given birth to her oldest niece, Dana knew she had to take a leap of faith. She wanted to tell her niece (now nieces) to follow her calling and do everything she could to make her dreams come true. She found an international school where she could teach, packed her bags, not knowing anyone, and moved across the world.

She ended up living and teaching there for four years. It was the most amazing experience of her life! She dreams of retiring there one day.

In writing this book, she hopes that you enjoy learning about Egypt as much as she has and that one day you'll find a place in the world that makes you want to learn everything there is to know about it.